Cash: More is Better!

Plug the Cash Leaks in Your Business

Fred Pieplow

The opinions expressed in this manuscript are solely the opinions of the author and do not represent the opinions or thoughts of the publisher. The author has represented and warranted full ownership and/or legal right to publish all the materials in this book.

Cash: More is Better!
Plug the Cash Leaks in Your Business
All Rights Reserved.
Copyright © 2014 Fred Pieplow
v2.0

Cover Photo © 2014 JupiterImages Corporation. Author's Photo: www.maryjohnsonphotography.com. All rights reserved - used with permission.

This book may not be reproduced, transmitted, or stored in whole or in part by any means, including graphic, electronic, or mechanical without the express written consent of the publisher except in the case of brief quotations embodied in critical articles and reviews.

Outskirts Press, Inc.
http://www.outskirtspress.com

ISBN: 978-1-4787-2902-0

Outskirts Press and the "OP" logo are trademarks belonging to Outskirts Press, Inc.

PRINTED IN THE UNITED STATES OF AMERICA

Read this book if you are the owner or manager of a business that:

1. is in a cash flow crunch,
2. cannot make sense of the advice from your Controller or CPA,
3. has a big financial decision to make,
4. is busier than it has ever been, but is not making money like it should,
5. is stuck and you need some new ideas, or
6. just wants some new insight into how business really works.

MiQuest 2014 Coach of the Year

On June 17, 2014 Fred Pieplow was honored as the Coach of the Year at the MiQuest Awards event. MiQuest supports the Michigan entrepreneurial culture by sponsoring two business plan competitions each year. Kevin Suboski, MiQuest Coach and Mentor Advocate, said that "coaches should support and nurture the intentionality and passion the entrepreneurs bring" to the competition. He also said: "we pick a coach that exemplifies the best of what a coach does." Almost 300 entrepreneurs from throughout Michigan registered to participate in this competition. See www.MiQuest.org for more information.

This book is dedicated to all the business owners who are doing what they love – filling a need and solving problems for their customers. They work long hours, risk their personal assets, and lay it all on the line for their business. Running a business is hard work. My hope is that this book can provide some ideas to get the cash moving again when times are tough.

Table of Contents

Introduction vii

Chapter 1: How Cash Works 1

Chapter 2: What Makes the Cash Flow? 9

Chapter 3: Value Added 33

Chapter 4: Operating Expenses 53

Chapter 5: Investment 65

Chapter 6: Manage Better 69

Chapter 7: Personal Reflections on Decisions 77

Introduction

Written for Small and Medium-Sized Companies.

As the owner or a manager of a company, have you ever been just plain stuck and out of ideas? The purpose of writing this is to provide the owner or manager of a small business with a list of things to consider for those times when running the business is just plain tough, or when the business needs some new thinking!

Many of the businesses I work with were started by entrepreneurs with a passion for delivering products and services in their specialty area. Little did they know that they would also need to be a part-time human resources manager, bookkeeper, purchasing agent, shipping and receiving clerk, and new product developer. With so many hats being worn, it is often very difficult to be a good time manager, to feel confident in the quality of your work, and think about growing your business, all at the same time.

There are many, many books written on being a better manager. Most of them are written for very large companies with very large data sets, years of historical records, and competitive analysis. There are also many books written on starting a new venture. These include how to write a business plan, and how to secure venture capital or other early types of funding vehicles.

There are far fewer books written for where most small businesses are-that is: the business is already started, has an income stream, and wants to improve its practices. Most businesses will never be the next Apple, or the next Procter & Gamble, or even the next high-growth company to capture all the headlines. Most businesses are trying to grow profitably and stay one step ahead of the competition. Most businesses are privately held with just one owner, or very few people owning stock.

This is written for that company. The Edward Lowe Foundation calls it a Stage 2 company. Stage 2 companies have been around for more than a year, have a revenue stream, and are basically stable. Their web site (www.edwardlowe.org) describes it like this:

> "Second-stage companies are those that have grown past the startup stage but have not yet grown to maturity. They have enough employees to exceed the comfortable control span of one owner/CEO and benefit from adding professional managers, but they may not have a full-scale professional management team.
>
> "A business typically begins to enter its second stage when it approaches $1 million in total receipts. The transition process may continue until it hits $100 million in receipts, although for most companies $50 million represents the upper limit of second stage. By $100 million, a firm will have to be professionally managed in order to continue to thrive and grow and be in its third stage of development. Employee numbers and revenue ranges vary by industry, but the population

of firms with 10 to 100 employees and/or $750,000 to $50 million in receipts includes the vast majority of second-stage companies."

The economic development community does not get excited about them, newspapers ignore them, and there are few tax breaks for the Stage 2 company. They are boring...but they represent the majority of businesses in the USA.

Often the CEO or president did not set out to lead an organization. They have a technical expertise that drove them to develop a unique solution in the marketplace, and the company came along with it. Perhaps they are family and either they feel forced into a leadership role in the company, or that role is their best career option, even if their background is not related to their role.

Some writers want you to believe that if you just follow their X Step Process you will achieve your life goals. My experience is that running a business is hard work. It takes diligence, planning, risk taking, and making complex decisions with incomplete data under extreme time pressures to make a business work. Just when you think you have it figured out...change happens and you have to figure it out all over again. There is no one right answer that works in all circumstances for any size business every time. That is why you, the owner/manager, must constantly review where you are, decide where you want to go, and develop and execute plans to get moving in the right direction.

> **Running a business is hard work. 'Nuff said!'**

Another critical aspect of small, usually privately held, companies is that they tend to change the majority owner every thirty years or so. Sometimes, that is a smooth transition, often to another family member. Sometimes, however, no buyer can be found, and the business struggles to survive or eventually collapses.

> **Don't just add value to your business...find ways to multiply value in your business!**

If you are an owner or manager of a Stage 2 company, this book is for you. I hope there are one or more concepts in the book that you can put up on the white board, brainstorm how it might work for you, and develop a plan to move your company to a higher performance level.

Frequently Asked Questions:

Here is a short list of the questions I get asked over and over again. Perhaps you have asked one or more of these yourself.

1. Why does it seem that the better the business is, the less cash we have? Conversely, when business slows down, cash seems to pile up. How can that be?

    Look for a discussion on this in Chapter 2 – Cash Out.

2. When my highest margin product is flying off the shelf, we make less money. How can that be?

    It's all about managing your biggest constraint! See Chapter 2 – Mix Matters for a discussion of this topic.

3. My Cost Accountant says our new product won't cover enough overhead to be worth the investment. My gut says it will be good for us. What am I missing?

    Ask your Cost Accountant to show you the value your customer sees in your overhead. Major hint: there isn't any! Look in Chapter 2 – New Product Decision for more discussion of how overhead affects product-level decision making.

4. We have completed several cost savings events. Why haven't we seen the results on the bottom line?

    Another constraint management question. Check out Chapter 4 – Reduce Your Cost to see what is really going on here.

5. What is the biggest mistake entrepreneurs make regarding cash management?

> Oh my! It is hard to narrow this down. Look throughout the book for hints, and check out Chapter 6 for my short list.

One more thing...*Cash: More Is Better* is NOT about the mindless pursuit of more. In the Bible, Paul says "For the love of money is a root of all kinds of evil" (1Timothy 6:10a). Money by itself will not solve problems. In fact, having money allows you to ignore problems you would not tolerate if there was no cash. This is about getting your policies, procedures, and strategies out of the way of maximizing cash throughout your organization.

When this happens, you achieve flexibility, being able to choose to do or not to do certain things. Activities like training, attending conferences, advertising, innovation, and sales prospecting get cut when budgets are tight. These multiply the value of the business – not just add value. These increase employee engagement, encourage risk-taking, and allow you to give the customer more than the minimum required by your agreement. This flexibility allows you to operate internally and externally in the "WOW" arena, where employees want to work and invite their friends to work there too. This "WOW" factor creates intensely loyal customers who share their experience with others.

It sometimes takes a little cash to get to and maintain the "WOW" feeling. That is why it is so important to stop the cash leaks wherever they are. Because as we all know, when it comes to **Cash: More Is Better!**

CHAPTER 1

How Cash Works

When times get tough, the tough business person figures out a way to keep things going. Economists may argue as to when a recession starts and when a recession is over, but most business owners would agree that times are tougher now (2014) than before the beginning of the recession of 2008. There always seems to be a so-called expert predicting that regular gas will be above $5.00 per gallon in the summer, and oil-based products will cost more. Not to mention that steel will cost more, and health care will cost more (okay, health care really will cost more!). Also, credit will be tight and unemployment will remain high. Some of these undoubtedly will come to pass, but somehow well-managed organizations get through crisis after crisis. The government here in the USA seems to be adding to the uncertainty. Now may or may not be a time for bold moves in your business, but it certainly is a time for conserving cash and accelerating cash flow where you can.

Paul Simon's song described "Fifty Ways to Leave Your Lover," but in fact, you only need to use one. Once you "hop on the bus" you do not need "to be coy," "make a new plan" or "slip out the back."

Similarly, this list may give you forty-nine ideas that you cannot use at the moment, but one good idea will be worth your time. And who knows, an idea that may not be right today could be just the trick tomorrow. It is my hope that as your circumstances change, you refer to these pages and the web site www.cashmib.com often and discover that kernel of an idea that jump-starts your organization in a better direction.

Improving the operating performance of your company can be organized into three main areas:

1. Increasing Value Added (similar to Gross Margin, Revenue less the direct cost of delivering the product or service)

2. Reducing Operating Expenses (the rest of the cost of doing business for the period)

3. Reducing Investment (Working Capital and Fixed Assets, the money tied up in business)

> More Value Added is good.
> Less Operating Expense is good.
> Less Investment is good.

This follows the philosophy of the Theory of Constraints as developed by Eli Goldratt in his book *The Goal*, and many other books and writings. Constraint management will be explained briefly later. Dr. Goldratt used the term Throughput (T); I use Value Added. They are equivalent terms, I just think that Value

HOW CASH WORKS

Added is more understandable, representing the unique contribution the company makes to the value chain it serves.

Think of these cash-generating ideas as tools in the tool box. Just like a home repair project, using the wrong tool can be dangerous and may not fix the problem. Before we discuss the tools themselves, it is important to discuss how cash flows in, through, and out of the business, so that the right tool can be applied at the right time to achieve the desired results.

Business models matter, and there are many books that discuss model issues. I will deal only with business models here as they reflect on how cash flows through the business. We will explore retail, wholesale, contract manufacturing, and proprietary product manufacturing here.

How Cash Works

Cash is neutral. It does not discriminate. It does not care where it came from or where it is going.

> **Cash is neutral.**

It has no perspective of time. It is not loyal; you can get it from one revenue source and spend it on a different part of the business. Once you have it, you have complete control of what you will accomplish with it.

This is important-please allow me to explain. Let's say you work at a manufacturing company. Your sales staff says you are missing a significant amount of work because you do not have a machine capable of performing a specific task. The machine needed costs $250,000 and will have a monthly payment of

◄ CASH: MORE IS BETTER!

$5,000 if you lease it. Your Cost Accountant will ask you how much floor space it will take up so he can allocate building depreciation and other factory overhead. The Cost Accountant will want to know how many pieces will be made, how much direct and indirect labor will be added, and so on. All that information is interesting, but can mislead the owner/manager into believing that the simple act of adding this machine will reduce costs on other products. Unless you are fortunate enough to have fixed contractual commitment from a reputable company that guarantees you the volume of parts to be made on this machine, you are taking a risk that you will be able to achieve a positive cash contribution to the company by adding this machine.

Your Cost Accountant will tell you to allocate building and other supposedly fixed costs to parts run on this machine. So, I assume that the Cost Accountant will then go back and reduce the cost allocated to all the other parts produced in the building. If so, a part that had a cost of $10 now has a cost of $9 and nothing was done to change the process or supply chain on that part. As Eli Goldratt would say, "REEEEAAAALLY?" What a bunch of goofiness. Please look at the chart below to see the explanation of how costs work in the REAL world.

Often the Cost Accountant will suggest you move production of a part from an old (paid for) machine to a new machine to get more overhead coverage. How silly is that? Unless the customer is going to pay more, or total costs will go down, this accomplishes absolutely nothing.

Chart 1.1

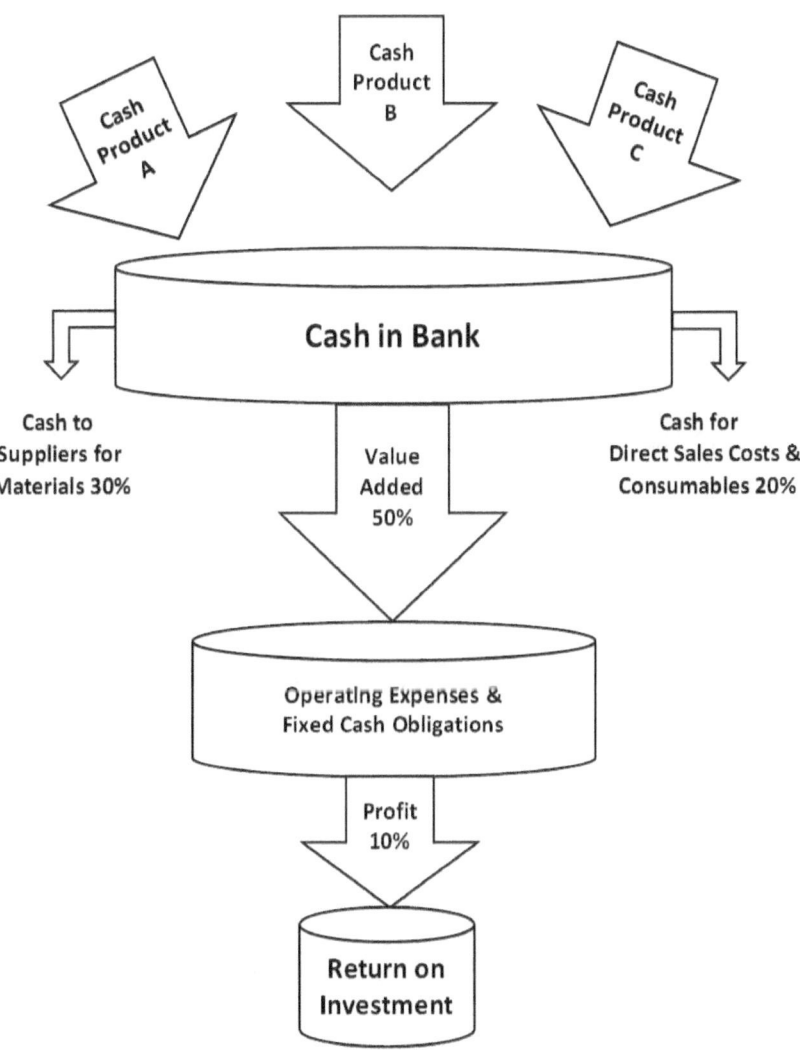

◀ CASH: MORE IS BETTER!

The reality is that buying this machine adds $5,000 to the monthly cash obligations of the company, period. The leasing company does not care whether you make parts on the machine or not. It wants you to make your monthly payment – on time. You may have to hire people and/or train them to work on the machine; they expect to be paid regardless of the volume of parts made on the machine.

Now it is up to you and your sales team to bring in business to the company which results in more than an additional $5,000 per month in Value Added to pay for the additional cash obligation (the lease). It does not matter whether this machine ever is used; the cash obligation has been increased. Obviously, you want to have the new machine functioning and making parts, but it really does not matter to cash flow what the source of Value Added is. There must be enough Value Added to cover Operating Expenses and the demands on Investment.

In my experience and observations, five truisms about cash have revealed themselves to me. I am sure you will see them is many forms throughout the book.

Five Laws of Cash

1. Cash is neutral. It does not know where it came from and it will go wherever you send it.

2. Spending cash on something that will get sold multiplies its value.

3. Spending cash on something that expires like electricity or taxes does not add value to a product.

4. Lazy cash (old receivables, inventory, and assets) tends to decrease in value over time.

Finally, Cash: More Is Better!

Chapter 1 Review Questions:

1. What is the Value Added for each major revenue source in your organization?

2. Do you understand the value of the overhead applied at each work center?

3. Do you have "Lazy Cash" in your organization?

CHAPTER 2

What Makes the Cash Flow?

Anyone who has started a new business understands the almost undeniable truth in the old adage "It takes money [or time!] to make money." Even if you have an incredibly good idea that is easy to understand and everyone agrees it is a great idea, vendors will want money up front, as you have no payment history. Bankers will not lend money without collateral, and investors will want a significant percentage of ownership for joining in the early risk of a new venture.

Friends and family are often the first to sign on to help the new start-up. They can be the most patient of investors, waiting a long time to get their money back and lending money sometimes on just a handshake. There is an additional risk associated with borrowing from friends and family. That risk is losing the relationship should there be difficulty in paying them back as agreed, or even a misunderstanding on how the money is to be used. When you borrow or accept an investment from friends and family, be sure to write things down and then follow up often with news about the business to avoid unnecessary conflicts.

It is difficult for an easy-to-understand idea to get off the ground, so you can imagine the difficulty in starting up a business with a revolutionary technology or new business model. The more proven your business model is, the easier it will be to convince the lender or investor to get on your team. Having customers who are paying money for your service or product is the truest test to validate the business model. With an active customer base, the main question is scale; can the business grow to meet the goals in your business plan?

There are many books and articles written on getting investors on your team, and this effort is not about that. This writing starts with the assumption that you have a business that has customers and cash is flowing. Now the challenge is to use the limited resource, cash, to the biggest benefit for your company. In the long run this must be done without alienating your supply chain, bankers, and investors, so it must be done carefully. The other consideration that we will discuss is the impact on the market. Most small companies deal in a relatively small section of a larger market, and care must be taken not to jeopardize your place in that market unintentionally (intentionally is a totally different matter!). We will discuss intentionally changing your place in the market, but we always must consider negative reactions to any moves that we make by our competitors that will undermine the plans we have. With that in mind, here is a discussion of how cash flows through a business.

WHAT MAKES THE CASH FLOW?

Cash Out

On the surface, cash out seems the easiest to understand and define. There is inventory to buy, payroll to meet, loan obligations to pay, equipment to maintain, and so on. It is interesting to note that for most small businesses, revenue tends to increase on a relatively even pace over time, while costs go up in a stair-step fashion. Many companies close their eyes and believe that cash will be there when they need it if sales are strong enough. This belief system often works when things are relatively stable and your planned Value Added covers your planned operating expenses.

However, when there's a dramatic increase in sales, which means more inventory to buy and more labor to pay, usually before the customer's money comes back at you, which can cause a strain on cash. Another interesting observation is that, when sales drop dramatically, to manage your business

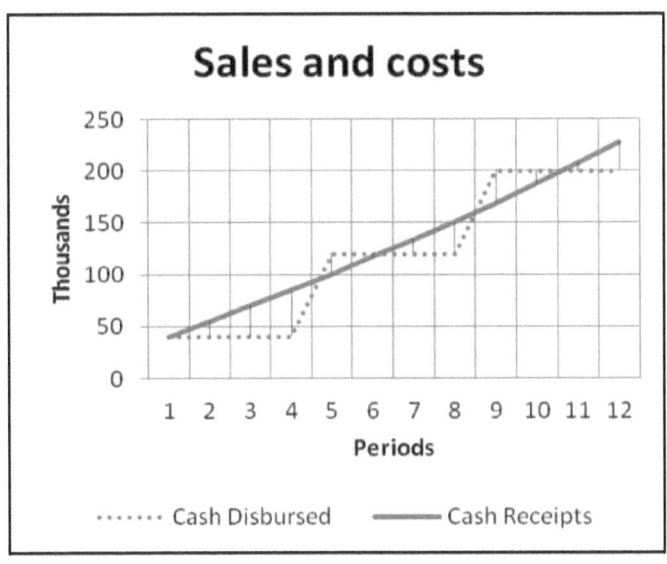

CASH: MORE IS BETTER!

properly you will put the brakes on making new inventory, which reduces your cash out. For a short period of time cash actually increases. Many small business people who have not experienced this phenomenon get deluded into thinking that things are better than they really are because there's more money in the checking account than they are accustomed to seeing. This is an extremely dangerous time for small business, because that money is often spent on other items rather than getting ready for the next spike in sales (which hopefully is soon to follow).

Many times when cash gets tight, companies manage through that cycle by delaying payments to their vendors. This is often justified by saying "My customer's delaying their payment to me; therefore I must delay my payment to you." It is often believed that this is an unavoidable consequence, especially if your customer base is notoriously slow paying. However, if you expect your suppliers to continue to support you, and deliver to you under sometimes extraordinary circumstances, you must maintain a great relationship with them. Meeting your commitments to your suppliers affords you the privilege of leaning on them when the need arises. If you have an opportunity to make a sale and beat your competitor in a new way, having your supplier willing to expedite shipping or whatever meets your needs on this significant new piece of business is a great asset. If you make it easy for your suppliers to sell to you and you meet your commitments to them, when those circumstances arise, the great suppliers will go to bat for you. If you're always late on payments, and are a tough customer to

WHAT MAKES THE CASH FLOW?

deal with in other ways, it will be harder for the vendor to do the extraordinary for you.

Communication is the best way to develop this type of relationship with a key supplier. Keeping them in the loop with both good news and bad news develops trust and earns the right to ask for accommodations. This transparency can transform the relationship from transactional to inter-dependency, where even a big company supplier to a small company values the long-term relationship and loyalty developed between the two organizations. Anyone can buy something from a company. Creating an intentional inter-dependency with a supplier or with a customer creates a commitment for a service level that competitors stuck in the transaction mode will find hard to copy.

In dealing with anyone who is a stakeholder in your business, maintaining the integrity of the company is incredibly important. Following the phrase "tell them what you are going to do-then do what you told them" will pay dividends over and over when your company gets into a tight cash position. For example, if you are forced to be late on a payment to a supplier, contacting them and telling them when you will be able to make that payment goes a long way to maintaining a great relationship. When you do that, over time a trust relationship is built that has a great value. Missing the commitment for the second or third time erodes that trust. Dr. Stephen Covey, author of *The Seven Habits of Highly Successful People*, calls that the balance in the "Emotional Bank Account." Transactions that work make deposits that build the account balance. Missing a commitment reduces the balance – and

CASH: MORE IS BETTER!

deductions happen a lot faster than deposits. Overdrawing the account can cause irreparable harm between the companies. Dr. Covey's context was at an individual level, but the same applies to companies, because after all, companies are made up of people!

You make and keep your company's integrity by making and keeping commitments. To do this, it is important to understand how cash flows through your business, which will be discussed next.

Cash In

The cash collection process varies from business to business. In a retail operation, cash is usually exchanged at the time of sale. In a business where equipment is made to order, the customer may be required to make a significant prepayment before the vendor will ship the order. For many businesses, the market requires purchasing raw materials, adding labor and any other forms of Value Added, shipping the product, and then waiting thirty days or more for the customer's money to come back to you. Whatever your business model, projecting and proactively managing the cash coming back to you from your customer is critical in managing your business.

Here is a brief discussion of some of the common cash management techniques used by small businesses and loved by their bankers.

Methods of Managing Cash

13-Week Cash Flow

This is a detailed projection of both the cash coming into the business and the cash commitments made by the business over the next quarter. This is a great planning tool to manage business and to communicate to your stakeholders (the bank) what to expect in the coming months. It requires an in-depth understanding of Accounts Receivable and any other form of collections that will increase cash in the time period. You must also look at your Accounts Payable, payments on the long-term debt obligations, insurance payments (which are often quarterly), commissions, payroll and payroll taxes, state and federal tax payments, and any other obligations the company has made. A well-done 13-week cash flow will often show negative cash available in certain weeks. That is exactly the purpose of the effort and allows the company and the bank to manage any credit line needs they may have, or the company to chat with its vendors if they're going to need extra time to meet their obligations for a short period of time.

Accounts Receivable Aging

One piece to the cash flow puzzle is Accounts Receivable. Every good accounting package provides an Accounts Receivable aging. There are a few options, such as aging from the invoice date or the due date; those can be selected based on your specific

CASH: MORE IS BETTER!

circumstances. The point is to look at your open invoices to your customers, and help them pay you according to terms. There are some variances based on the type of business. Some businesses have a few large invoices in a month, while others issue many small invoices.

Managing receivables with many small invoices can be tedious, and you must make it easy for your customers to pay, such as offering credit card payment. When your business has a few large invoices, again you must make it easy for your customer to pay. Large invoices tend to have predictable approval cycles in the customer's organization. One method I have found effective is to contact the customer's payables department a few weeks before the invoices are due to see if all the approvals have been obtained. If they have not been obtained, I try to find out what is left open and contact the responsible party to close that issue. The best way to do this is to maintain a great relationship with the folks in the Accounts Payable Department at your customer's business. Don't just call in when they are late and scream at them by telling them all the problems they're causing you. Contact them early with a friendly "Hey, can you help me out?" and most of the time they will give you the information you need to manage your cash. That does not mean they will stop what they're doing to write you a check, but it does mean you should be able to get the information you need to predict when their payment will be made under normal circumstances.

One way to keep your invoices at the top of the Accounts Payable pile is to offer a discount for prompt payment. There are many forms of discounting, so don't overly complicate it. The important thing with discounting is to be tough when your customer pays after the discount period but takes the discount anyway. This creates all kinds of bad habits at the customer level, and makes taking the discount away difficult.

Accounts Payable Aging

Similar to Accounts Receivable, most accounting packages are capable of telling you when an obligation will be due in the future if you have set it up properly. This is important documentation for both yourself and the bank to ensure you have not missed any significant cash obligations. One warning here: many items that put a strain on cash do not go through Accounts Payable. These items include payroll and payroll taxes, some insurance payments, sales commissions, and many other items that get paid outside of the normal Accounts Payable cycle. This is neither good nor bad; it is just something to be aware of.

Cash-to-Cash Cycles

Most businesses that have been around for a while have a fairly predictable cycle of cash in and cash out. It is <u>extremely</u>

CASH: MORE IS BETTER!

important to understand the cash cycle of your business. One significant determining factor of the cash cycle is length of time between the time your customer makes their decision to buy and the amount of time your supply chain requires to deliver your product. For example, if your customer expects delivery in two weeks, and you have parts that take four weeks to complete, you need to manage inventory to meet the customers' demands. Here is a brief discussion of two types of Cash to Cash Cycles.

Sell Cycle Shorter than the Buy Cycle – Results in: Higher Inventory, Higher Margins, Higher Risks.

> Many businesses operate in this environment. In retail, customers want what they want when they want it, which is immediately. If the retailer does not have the item on the shelf, many times they will go to another retail outlet. This is especially true of online sales. Many items can be shipped the same day or the next day and consumers are willing to wait for the delivery person to show up with their product. In other circumstances, waiting 24 hours is just too long. In many business-to-business markets, the customer will wait as long as two weeks from the time they make their purchasing decision to receive their product. However, the supply chain cycle might take six weeks from order to finished goods availability. Therefore, the supplier must maintain inventory based on a forecast of what the market will demand. The accuracy of this forecast will often play a huge role in the company's ability to manage their working capital. The more the company

WHAT MAKES THE CASH FLOW?

understands about the constraints in their supply chain, the better their ability to manage inventory and meet their customer's expectations. There is a brief discussion on constraint management following.

Sell Cycle Longer than the Buy Cycle – Results in: Low Inventory, Make to Order, Lower Margins, Lower Risks.

Some businesses are in a market where the customer will wait 6 to 8 weeks for a product. If the longest lead time part included takes 4 weeks to make, the supplier can maintain low inventories and manage staffing to meet demand. My observation is that this circumstance does not maintain itself for very long. Competitors will promise shorter lead times, or those pesky customers will start to delay their decisions and your own sales people will promise shorter lead times to get a sale. Sooner than later, the promised lead time tends to match the best-case scenario of your ability to deliver.

Constraint Management

Every business has constraints. Without constraints, sales would rise to the size of the market. It is

> Stop being EFFICIENT!
>
> (Unless you are effective too!!)

extremely important to understand the constraints on the business, including understanding the biggest constraint. By definition, every company has a "biggest" constraint. The point is not to eliminate the biggest constraint, but to manage it and to maximize the Value Added at the constraint. In his book *The Goal*, Eli Goldratt describes how a manufacturer can define and manage the constraint.

Very briefly, if you have a workstation, or a supplier, who can provide fewer units than your market requires, that is a constraint. Increasing the capacity of a non-constraint work station does nothing to improve your Value Added if the constraint remains constant. If you increase the capacity of the constraint by 10%, you usually increase the ability of the company to increase Value Added by about the same percent.

Mix Matters

Many times I get asked by the owner of the business about why he's not making money. Sales of his highest-margin product are through the roof-he cannot make them fast enough, yet the profits just aren't there.

Invariably, when we dig into the numbers we discover that the constraint in his system is controlling the amount of Value Added available to the company. This is always the case and follows the laws of physics. By definition, every business has a biggest constraint. Managing that constraint is usually the difference between success and failure of a business. Please allow me to give an example of how this works.

Your company has two products, product A and product B. Product A has a Value Added of 80% while

WHAT MAKES THE CASH FLOW?

product B's Value Added is only 30%. Market demand for a maximum of 6 product A's and 21 product B's per day. Therefore, you put all your resources and craft your incentive plans around selling six product A's per day. This leaves two hours of production time available per day to make and sell product B. This follows every piece of logic you have ever been taught, yet things just aren't working out as we had planned.

In the following table, you can see the basic facts as described above:

Measure	Product A	Product B
Price per unit	$1,000	$1,000
Materials and other direct costs	200	700
Value Added per unit	800	300
Value Added as a percent of Sales	80%	30%
Time at the constraint per unit	1 hour	20 minutes
Maximum Value Added per 8-hour day	$6,400	$9,000
Value Added per hour at the constraint	$800	$900

Your plan above yields $6,400 per day of total value-added. This result is from selling six product A's per day for a Value Added of $4,800 (six units X $800 per unit) plus product B's Value Added of $1,800 (6 units X $300). Your instinct is that you can do better.

The key measure is Value Added over time at the constraint. Product B yields more Value Added per hour than product A. If you were to meet the demand available for product B of 21 units per day, product B would provide $6,300 (21 units X $300) of Value Added. You now have one hour per day available at the constraint to make product A. This will provide an additional $800 (I unit X $800) of Value Added. Your total Value Added in this plan is now $7,100 per day. That is $500 per day higher than selling out with the product that yields a higher margin percentage.

It really is just that simple.

Maximizing Value Added at the constraint must be the goal of the organization. Therefore it is critical that you identify the biggest constraint of your organization. You also need to understand the Value Added available from every product or service available to your team, and how much time each of those products or services requires from the constraint. Finally, you need to understand the market demand for each product or service. Now you have all the information necessary to maximize the effectiveness of your organization. It is critical that you look at your policies and procedures to make sure that everything you do is focused on maximizing Value Added at the constraint. Look at your sales commission plans, plant production incentives, marketing time and materials, etc. to determine if all those efforts align with your maximum potential Value Added by product line.

Mix Matters.

Efficiency vs Effectiveness

STOP BEING EFFICIENT! In the Theory of Constraints world, traditional efficiency measures can be dangerous. If you are working better and better at a process that is less and less important to your business, what good is it? Unless you are working at the constraint, Efficiency is a measure of Operating Expenses, not a way to improve Value Added. Think about it. If you are working at workstation A that is not the constraint, and you improve the process from 8 hours per unit to 7 hours per unit (a 12.5% improvement!), what value have you created? If you cannot take that hour and apply it in a productive way elsewhere in the business, it is a mythical savings. Often, work rules, habits, and just the ruts we all get into prevent those local improvements from reaching the bottom line.

Effectiveness, on the other hand, drives savings from process improvements to the bottom line. Using the same example as above, if workstation A _IS THE CONSTRAINT_, that same 12.5% increase allows more product to be available for sale in the same period of time and _will increase the overall Value Added_ of the organization.

Early Warning Systems

Many businesses have a rhythm that seems to repeat on a fairly regular basis. Even in a seasonal business, there should be benchmarks for orders received by a certain date, or for sales completed by a certain date. The type of warning system that is significant to you will vary depending on the type of business model you are in. If your industry has a relatively standard benchmark that everyone seems to use, such as cases sold, units ordered, backlog in dollars or units, or time per unit of measure, you know where you stand at all times compared to that measure.

Early warnings can be either for revenue indicators or for major cost drivers. In the automotive industries, days of inventory on hand at the manufacturer is an indicator not only for their production, but for their suppliers, their suppliers' suppliers, their dealers, service departments, the rental companies, repair shops, used car dealers, and more. Many buyers use commodities futures as an indicator of both price and availability to help time their purchases.

The problem with standard benchmarks as an early warning system is that if everyone is using them, they are of little or no strategic value. Everyone will see a change signaled at exactly the same time – making it hardly an early warning. What will create strategic value is an early warning indicator that no one else is using.

Types of Early Warning Systems

Some simple Early Warning Systems include:

- Commodity purchases: futures pricing.

- Back Order businesses: level of back orders at a certain date, back order trend line.

- International purchases: governmental actions to curb or encourage imports or exports.

- Technology: anticipated leapfrog announcements.

- Tourism and retail: travel issues.

If you see someone who seems to be consistently beating the competition to a certain point, they may have found a warning bell no one else is listening to.

New Product Decision

Any time you are considering adding a new product, you need to consider all the ways it will affect your business. How many people, if any, will you need to add? How will it affect the capacity at your constraint? Will it move your constraint? Those are just some of your production issues.

In the market, you must discern what value this brings for you to your existing customers. Will it bring in a totally new customer base, and will those customers then increase demand of your existing offering? Are we confident that we can complete all the required steps for a cost less than the value offered to the customer? If we are attracting a new customer base, just how will we reach them?

Does this effort add risk to our current markets? For example, if we currently are a premium product, will a discounted version diminish the value of current products in the eyes of the customer? What direction is this product going in the market? How can we impact that direction in our favor?

CASH: MORE IS BETTER!

Big note: this is NOT an introspective by the accounting department. This should be a collaborative effort by all the departments affected to achieve maximum buy-in and enthusiasm for the new initiative. Much of the effort that goes into answering these questions requires judgment.

For the numerical analysis, here are issues that need to be dealt with.

- Number of units per period
- Price per unit
- Variable Cost to deliver: Materials, Discounts, Commissions, Consumables, and more
- Effect on the Constraint
- Changes in Operating Expenses, such as: Engineering, Facilities, Marketing, Indirect Sales Costs, and so on
- Investments needed, such as: Equipment, increase in Inventory, and Accounts Receivable

When you have all the data in neat rows and columns, you can do some analysis.

1. Value Added (Estimated Sales less the Variable Costs to Deliver) by product.

2. If your constraint is time at a work station, calculate Value Added per hour (or other time unit) at the constraint.

3. The net effect on the business is Value Added plus or minus the change in Operating Expenses, and plus or minus the change in Investment. You can check this out per constraint unit also.

This is a good way to compare new product opportunities. By estimating a five-year projection for the analysis, you get to see the short- and long-term effects a new product may have on the business. A new product that puts a lot of stress on the cash flow in the early years may be the cash cow you are looking for in the future.

Estimated Value Added for the Product.

The same data needed above for comparing new product opportunities can be used to look at current operations. You should estimate the direct variable cost of delivering the new product at various volume levels. Remember, the direct variable costs include items like material, consumables, discounts, sales commissions, and other costs incurred only because we are making this sale.

A unit sales projection then needs to be made for the shorter of the life of the product, or five years. This provides enough time to see the effect of the product maturing without requiring blue sky projections for the distant future.

Once you have a sales forecast for the projection period, you can do the math to determine the Value Added estimate for the product. You can compare that to the

◄ CASH: MORE IS BETTER!

Value Added for your other products. If you are accustomed to getting a 60% Value Added (as compared to the sales price) and this product is forecasted to yield only 40%, you have some more thinking to do.

In addition to the Value Added, you must consider any changes to Operating Expenses. Any change to operating expenses that occurs solely because of this decision, need to be included in the cash analysis. For example, if you will need to add an engineer and two customer support personnel, all the costs associated with adding those people need to be considered. Conversely, if this decision will eliminate the rental of a machine or eliminate an outside service, that cost reduction should be included in the benefit of making this decision.

Constraint Decision-making

Rewarding proper behavior means you need to define proper behavior! The first step is to educate the entire organization on how the constraint affects the success of the business as a whole, and how their work can maximize the constraint. Two examples:

1. A manufacturer of custom metal products has observed that the welding department is a constraint. Adding welding capacity is a relatively inexpensive process – if you can find qualified welders. That "if" became a stumbling block, so they examined their processes and observed that their welding steps included getting raw material to work on, quality control, and deburring sharp edges (a relatively easy task). To increase their welding capacity, they moved the

raw material set-up from welding to the prior cutting step (not the constraint) and moved the deburring to a support function. These two changes added about 20% to their welding capacity for much less added Operating Expense than a new welder would have cost. Even more important than the Operating Expense savings is adding capacity to the constraint to increase Value Added.

2. A professional services company has a process that involves about ten steps. Several of those steps require some level of experience to perform at a high level, and one step can only be done by the licensed professional. There is more work available than the one licensed professional can do, so the obvious solution is to make that step as efficient as possible. Everyone in the organization must subordinate their functions to be sure the licensed professional is <u>never waiting for work</u>. An hour lost by that position is an hour lost forever to the whole organization. Sometimes one of the other steps must be interrupted to keep the licensed professional busy. The owner of that process must not be punished for any inefficiency, nor can they let pride or ego keep them from subordinating their step in favor of assisting the licensed professional.

Business Models – from the perspective of Cash: connecting decisions to the Value Added of the business.

This chart shows typical business model characteristics of Value Added, Operating Expenses and Investment for various types of organizations.

Business Model Chart

Business Model Chart 1 of 2

Business Type	Source of Value Added	Investment	Risk	VA as a Percent of Sales	Cash In	Cash Out
Project Based Fixed Price or Cost +	Expertise, time, purchasing power, supply chain management.	Education, training, infrastructure.	Fixed price projects, capacity planning.	High.	Few, large invoices. Advance payments?	Large steps for Value Added. Steady for OE.
Recurring Revenue	Asset to share. Time.	Facility, software, staff.	Technology change. Market shift.	High.	Steady. Ramps up or down.	Steps with Investment and OE (Staff).
Retail	Inventory. Convenience. Easy to buy from.	Inventory. Facility.	Inventory. Market shifts. Supplier quality.	Low to medium.	Depends on traffic. Fickle consumer. Seasonal.	In advance for most Inventory costs, steady for OE (Staff) unless seasonal.
Proprietary Product Manufacturing	Product differentiator.	Varies.	Technology change. Market shift.	Medium to high.	Varies.	In advance most Inventory costs, steady for OE.

WHAT MAKES THE CASH FLOW?

Business Model Chart 2 of 2

Business Type	Source of Value Added	Investment	Risk	VA as a Percent of Sales	Cash In	Cash Out
Contract Manufacturing	Service & efficiency.	Specialized equipment and services. Quality control.	Investment in equipment. Customers buy equipment.	Medium to high.	Per piece revenue based on customer schedule.	Low Value Added, steady OE. High Equipment.
Distributor	Quick access to inventory.	Inventory, staff, supply chain.	Inventory. Market shifts. Supplier quality.	Low to medium.	Steady, based on client demands.	Low facilities costs, High Inventory if stocking, steady OE.
Fee For Service	Expertise & time.	Education, Training, Infrastructure.	Capacity management, staying current.	High	Steady, based on client demands.	Low Investment costs, steady OE.

VA = Value Added (Revenue less direct costs to make the sale, material, freight, commissions)
I = Investment (Inventory, Accounts Receivable, less Accounts Payable)
OE = Operating Expenses (Most direct labor and all the other costs to run the business)

Chapter 2 Review Questions

1. What are you doing to nurture your vendor relationships?

2. What is your biggest constraint?

3. Why is it important for you to understand your supply chain's biggest constraint?

CHAPTER 3

Value Added

Increase Value Added
Value Added = Sales less direct variable cost of sales

The first area, and often the easiest to achieve quick, short-term improvement, is here. This is similar to Gross Margin, except that overhead and most labor are NOT included. The only costs in this formula are the additional costs incurred because you made and shipped these parts to your customer. Note that we are NOT trying to increase sales; increasing Value Added is the objective.

Again, Value Added is the Price minus things like materials, items consumed in making the product, packaging, extra labor or some overtime, freight, sales commissions, and other costs you would NOT have incurred if the sale had not been made. Your CPA will call these the direct variable cost of the sale. Note that it does not include labor. Many Theory of Constraints advocates have observed that there is a base labor cost that acts more like a fixed cost in Operating Expense because there is a certain level of labor that a company tries really really hard to maintain. These people are hard to replace, have years of experience, and may have had significant training.

One more point here, we are talking about dollars, not percent. Increasing your calculated Value Added percent is nice, but increasing the volume of dollars of Value Added is the objective, because you can spend dollars.

Here are several approaches to increasing Value Added. Each one is basic common sense and may seem too simple even to list in a work like this. My experience is that when the pace is quick and stress is plentiful, common sense is anything but common.

Increase Value Added by Increasing the Spread (Margin) Between Price and Cost

More Value Added is almost always good, but it can be hard to achieve. Competitive pressures, market demands, training your sales team, and other issues sometimes slow the change process.

1. Increase the price. This would be obvious, if the market would allow it. Often in slow markets, this is not easy. You also must consider:

    - How long since your last increase? Everyone understands that costs go up. A good customer wants their supplier base to be successful so the suppliers will be there for the long haul. That being said, no one likes a price increase under any circumstances. Customers expect you to find improvements in your process to keep prices low and to work your own supply chain to avoid an increase.

- Ways to tie your changes to changes in your cost of materials (if that is a good thing).

- Competitor pricing: Changing the price is also the easiest thing for a competitor to copy. If you increase your price, that gives your competitor an opportunity to increase theirs too.

Remember, your costs do NOT determine the price; the market does. There are some things you can do to successfully implement an increase when you absolutely cannot avoid a price

> Your costs do NOT determine the price, the market does!

change. Communicate the reason for the change. Give your market some warning so they can stock up at the old price, or a special deal to continue at the old price if they commit to a certain volume. Give your best customers a special deal, if you can, to soften the blow to their budgets.

You need to answer two questions to determine your price:

   a. What is the most the market will pay for this?

b. Am I willing to make it for that amount?

So, if the market will pay $100 and my Value Added is $50, I am probably okay with that. If my Value Added is only $10, I might not be okay, depending on other issues, such as risk, volume, Value Added per constraint unit, trends in the market, and many other issues.

Lower Your Cost Per Unit (Costs Over Units Produced)

Cost per unit is affected by every step in your supply chain, not just those steps under your direct control. The conflict with the supply chain is often being loyal to a long-time supplier when an innovative approach presents itself. There is always a balance to be weighed before switching vendors. Loyalty isn't the real issue. It is the risk of performance of the new vendor vs. the known performance of the current supplier. I always try very hard to stay with an existing supplier with a good track record. However, if they are clearly beaten in the market, that is not my problem. They need to become more competitive. It is their responsibility to be the best resource available, and your responsibility is to make the best long-term decision for your company.

2. Consider inviting one or more of your suppliers you want to develop a deep, mutually beneficial relationship with to a meeting. Here you can discuss the process of getting your product or service to market and what everyone's role is. Then you can have a frank discussion of how to take time and/or costs out of the system. You might be surprised

at what your suppliers come up with to save money – and make your offering more competitive.

3. Consider having your customer provide the raw materials. This is common in many industries, and unheard-of in others. Your customer may have more buying power and get a larger discount than your company can achieve. If your company is struggling with working capital, they can solve this issue-at a cost, of course.

> **Are they a Supplier or a Partner?**
>
> Forming great relationships with suppliers is never easy, but it is important. As much as suppliers like to throw the "Partner" word around, they (and you) are looking out for their own best interests. So your job is to create a sense of <u>inter-dependency</u> with them. This locking of arms with you and your supplier for the long-term good of both organizations is one that your competitors will find hard to duplicate and give you both a sustainable advantage in the market.

4. Work with your vendors to find ways to take advantage of discounts or programs they have to reduce your costs. Ask, and ask again and again. Suggest ways your supplier can become more competitive. Look for ways to save by changing order size, delivery times, and combining shipments with other suppliers or other customers of that supplier. Brainstorm with one or more suppliers in the room together to get the ideas flowing. You need your vendors to be successful so they are there to give you support when you need it. Don't be piggish. Tough, but fair, is the buyer (and seller) I aim to be.

CASH: MORE IS BETTER!

5. Freight needs to be part of your calculations to determine your buying patterns. Buying twice per month instead of weekly may not only save money with the supplier, but also might create significant savings in freight costs. Suppliers today are adding surcharges for freight without getting them approved by you. If they have quoted a fixed, <u>delivered</u> price DO NOT allow this. That is a price increase. Force them to negotiate any additional fees with you.

6. Find or form a buying club to pool your purchasing power. This seems to work best for high-volume items that may be viewed as commodities, such as corrugated that is not branded, or for supply items.

Increase Efficiency (Number of Pieces Over Time – Usually Either Man Hours or Machine Hours)

7. Has your constraint moved recently? Are you set up to maximize the units produced at the largest constraint (bottleneck) of your operation? Understanding your constraints is the key to making good decisions.

   Every business has one constraint that is the biggest thing holding them back. Sometimes it is a physical issue inside the building, like a work cell, or it can be something outside your control like geography, weather, a license restriction, etc. The objective is to maximize the volume at the constraint.

   There are many books written about constraint management. One resource to start with is the founder of the Theory of Constraints' website: www.toc-goldratt.com, or just do a search on Theory of Constraints. One point is that making an investment to improve the efficiency at a non-constraint area might reduce Operating Expenses, but it will not improve Value Added. The only way to improve Value Added is to expand the capacity at the biggest constraint.

8. Look at how you are staffed and the schedules your employees keep.

> The objective is to maximize Value Added at the constraint.

As more and more work becomes automated, employees with higher math, reasoning, and computer skills are in greater demand. Community colleges and state workforce development organizations often have or can customize training programs to meet some of your needs. You may need to send people off to training or develop your own training to meet your specific needs.

Here are a few Ideas to manage your staff:

- Do you really need that second shift?

- Do you have jobs that are no longer needed?

- Is your staff cross-trained to go to where the work is?

- Do you have work rules that are no longer relevant and slow your process down? This happens a lot in facilities that have highly developed procedures. In facilities that are ISO registered, or have union

◄ CASH: MORE IS BETTER!

> work rules, once a process is written down, it can be a large, complex process to make a change. Please do not misunderstand. This is not a problem with ISO or unions...it is a people problem! People get stuck in systems, and management needs to be passionate about change and the improvements the change will make for everyone.

9. Look at your incentive programs. Do they reward the behavior you need now? For example, if your incentive and commission plans provide maximum rewards for your highest-margin product which takes a long time at the constraint, your staff will work hard to make and sell a product with a low Value Added per Constraint Unit value.

If you have not completed a serious review of your incentives at every level of your organization in a couple of years, you might be surprised at what people are doing compared to what you think they should be doing. This is especially true if you have recently realized that your constraint is NOT what you thought it was. When the constraint moves, every process in the organization needs to be reviewed to see if it is still relevant to the new reality.

For decades, aluminum die casting plants rewarded their operators on measures of pieces or pounds produced in a shift. There was little attention paid to a quality issue called porosity. For a part to function properly over its expected life, it must have certain characteristics. Die cast parts made under the proper conditions will have those characteristics. However, if the metal is not hot enough, or

VALUE ADDED ➤

the cast pressure is too low, the piece will have porosity-air pockets that weaken the part. Porosity is usually not found until other Value Added costs, such as machining, are added to the product. This could be days or weeks later, long after the shift has received their productivity incentive pay.

10. Ask your employees how to improve efficiency. They will almost always have ideas. They won't all be good ideas, but it is worth the effort to get employees involved.

Create an Idea Bank!

Okay it's just a suggestion box with a cooler name, but you get the point. An Idea Bank has deposit slips and review committees to set interest rates (rewards for good ideas), and a monthly or quarterly dividend payment for good ideas. Have a little fun with this. My experience is that several small awards given on a regular basis are enough to stimulate the idea machine within a company. After all, the real reward is the recognition you give when you hand out that gift card in front of fellow employees – priceless! Of course, if someone comes up with a million-dollar idea, you may need to consider something more than a gift card, but there will be enough cash to provide the reward in that case.

Always think "Continuous Improvement." Plant-wide, you should have a few measures you watch closely. Units per labor hour, pounds produced per hour, scrap, and on-time delivery are examples. In addition, individual work stations or teams can have job-specific measures. These measures should be used to target improvements and justify expenditures on improvements. Remember, improvements at a non-constraint area may not show bottom line improvement.

Increase Value Added by Increasing the Volume of Units Sold

> Lowering the price is the easiest thing for a competitor to copy.

A manufacturer once told me that volume cures a lot of ills. Another told me that volume covers a lot of sins.

1. Lower the price!

   Duh! Lowering the price always increases volume, and more volume is always good – right? Of course not. If you are in a market where the customers are just not buying, all price reductions do is make the eventual business recovery more difficult.

   The market will usually allow a price reduction, but be very careful not to convert your Value Added to a commodity. The last thing you want to do is start a price war in your market. Once this starts, it can be difficult to stop.

   Price reductions should be accompanied by some form of lesser offer or special bundle when you can.

2. Bundle your offering in ways attractive to your customer, but improve your Value Added at the same time. Years ago banks would offer a toaster to anyone who opened a new account with more than $25. I never understood what a

toaster had to do with a bank account, but I remember my parents bringing home a new toaster and being very proud of their new "free" appliance. Today most offers are more directly associated with the primary product of the supplier, such as:

- A bank will offer to add $100 to an account when you set up direct deposit through your employer. Most people do not change their direct deposit arrangement often, so they believe they create a long-term client relationship with their $100 investment.

- Car dealerships offer "Tires for Life." If you are going to own the car for a long time, and have the discipline to follow all their rules, this can save thousands of dollars over the life of the car and keep you coming to the service department and the showroom while you are waiting.

3. Unbundle your offering to allow your customer to buy only what they need at that time. Here is a statement you will hear from me over and over again: "Make it easy for your customer to do business with you!"

4. Review your Value Proposition (sometimes called the Unique Selling Point) to your market. Are you communicating your value compared to the competition's value? Are you helping your customer define their ROI for buying your product? When you diagnose the correct problem of your customer and understand the pain points, you

can communicate to your customer in a way that makes your product or service the obvious choice. See "Area of Innovation" later in this chapter.

5. Look at your policies. Do you make it easy for the customer to buy from you? Do your policies cause friction between you and the customer, or do they enhance the buying experience? If you need an approval for something, how long does it take for you to get a decision? Too long is a friction point.

Policy Friction

Recently I rented a tuxedo for our daughter's wedding from a major retail chain. I am sure you have seen their TV ads. However, I live in Michigan, more than an hour from their nearest store. As soon as the engagement was announced, I planned ahead and had them measure me for the tux when I was near one of their stores. When the tux style was selected, I called the store nearest the wedding site in Chicago to give them the measurements and order the tux. Easy, right? Well, they said, "You will have to come in to the store to be measured." I said, "I can't." They said again, "You will have to come in to the store to be measured." I said again, "I can't." Their first reason was because they had to be sure of the measurements. I told them I was measured at one of their stores. Eventually a supervisor said the real reason I had to come in was because they needed a deposit to order the tux. No problem. I said, "I have a credit card in my hand." He told me they did not take credit cards over the phone and I would have to come in to the store and make the deposit. I asked, "What century are you working in?" After being transferred two more times, the store manager flipped through some manual he dug out from the rubble on his desk and told me to try calling an 800 number they had for tux rentals. Here the gentleman was very professional, took my measurements, and was set up to handle a credit card by phone transaction. The tux was ordered, but I was angry and exhausted.

Can you see how this poorly communicated policy causes friction between the retailer and the customer? What policies does your organization have that cause friction in the sales process?

By the way, the wedding was spectacular, our daughter was radiant, and I did "like the way I looked!"

6. Examine your Area of Innovation. In *The Pumpkin Plan* by Mike Michalowicz the Area of Innovation is divided into three categories: Price, Quality, and Convenience. A company really competes in only one area. Choosing which area you will compete in and making all of your decisions

with that in mind allows you to focus your energies and reach a market in a spectacular way. By the way, that does not mean that you can ignore the other two categories. It just means that understanding what you are truly best at and energizing all your resources around that is the shortest route to success.

7. Consider running a "special price" with a limited time duration, limited number of products, special bundling, or other value differentiating package. Offers touting an "Inventory Reduction Sale" or a "Manager's Out of Town Sale" often seem desperate or cheesy. Depending on your market, a value approach will usually be more effective, and not ruin your position in the market. For Business to Business (B2B) sales especially, volume sales reduce costs and people understand that and might even appreciate the deal.

8. Check your product Value Added calculations to be sure you are covering all the costs you need to cover with any price change. If a new product is coming out or there is extreme cash pressure, you never want to sell below your direct cost. This results in negative Value Added. However, if product is getting stale, moving it now can be better than disposing of it at fire sale prices later.

   Some examples might be:

   - One for $100, two for $175;

   - Save 20% if you buy 100 units by March 1st; or,

- 15% off list if you buy our XYZ product from our in stock inventory by June 30.

9. <u>Add customers!</u> Again, this seems too simple to list, but at times you might be in a rut and feel you will never add a new customer again. This can easily happen in a relatively small market, such as selling to the North American integrated steel manufacturers (about six companies!). When this happens it is definitely time to leave your box. I mean get way out of your box! Think differently for a while. You need to consider the cost of acquiring a new customer – and the benefit of denying that customer to the competition! Also, is your offering really restricted to only one small market, or have you put an <u>artificial</u> limit on yourself?

> Example: One company I worked for sold large capital improvement projects to the steel and aluminum manufacturers, such as US Steel, Bethlehem Steel, and Alcoa. When Detroit was making cars, they could not make steel fast enough, and productivity was very important (and I looked pretty smart because my division did well). When Detroit slowed down or when China dumped steel in California, the steel makers stopped and reduced their capital improvement budgets to zero (and I looked dumb as a stump). Price did not matter; there was no traditional money to be had. So we created service contracts and diverted resources to other industries to get through the slow period.

◄ CASH: MORE IS BETTER!

> Over the years, companies that start out servicing one big client, such as the local Fortune 500 Company, often pay lip service to diversification. Everyone understands that having sales concentrated in one client, or even one industry is dangerous, but most get so busy feeding that client that they do not dedicate the resources to find new customers and markets. Then when the customer gets the flu, they get pneumonia.

10. Ask your sales people what is holding them back. If they respond with "Our minimum order quantity is too high," "It takes too long to approve the credit," "Our delivery times are too long," "Our product bundles do not meet customer needs," or other such comments – you have some work to do. Do not let a simple policy decision made in a different economy hold you back now. Dig into why those policies are what they are. Check into options on how to accomplish the same (or nearly the same) objective, but eliminate the obstacle.

11. Look at the map. What potential customers are in your sweet spot, or just outside of it, that you are not reaching? Look at your trade association data, talk to your truck drivers, etc. Find these customers, and make them a special limited time offer to give your product a try.

12. Offer a volume discount. This is a great way to lower the cost without lowering the price. It also locks your customer in so they achieve the discount. Most programs like this

involve purchases over weeks or months to achieve the discount. When the discount is achieved, a credit memo or other agreed-upon payment method completes the deal and locks in the customer relationship. Trips, dinners, sports tickets, and many other awards often sweeten the pot to get targeted players to work hard to move your products.

Add new products or services!

13. Talk to your customers. They often are having problems with a product or service similar to yours that would be a natural for your company. Customers are pretty smart people and have their own self-interest in mind. If they have a need that is not being met satisfactorily, there is an opportunity. Care must be taken not to step on a hornet's nest of problems, but often taking a fresh look at an existing problem results in a new solution.

14. Talk to your vendors. One may have a new product or service it is struggling to bring to a market you serve. Like customers, vendors have their own self-interest at heart, and significant due diligence is needed when helping a vendor solve a problem. Vendors may be looking to share costs more than to solve a customer's problem. Having said that, often you may have an entry for them into a market that they cannot seem to crack.

15. Talk to your sales people (I believe I said that before!). Listen for clues they have observed from sales calls, industry events, neighbors, church, and other interactions-even if they are unrelated to your industry. A good sales team is

◄ CASH: MORE IS BETTER!

always looking for ways to increase the top line. Depending on their incentive plans, they usually have a strong opinion on new products, pricing points, competition, policies, and other friction points in your system. Ask them which customers are expressing the most pain and why. This pain is your opportunity. Work closely with the sales team to be sure you both understand the need in the market, who else is working on meeting that need, and how you can differentiate yourself in that market. There is no substitute for your personal involvement here to make sure what your sales team is saying is the same thing their customers are telling them.

16. Get out of your box! Talk to your Chamber of Commerce, trade associations, bankers, and friends to see what they may be hearing and apply that to your situation and capabilities. The US Small Business Association (SBA at www.sba.gov) has many documents on their website to help the entrepreneur or manager. They also host webinars and local seminars to assist small business owners. Nationally there is the Small Business Development Center (SBDC), which has staff to assist the business owner in business planning, selling to the government, and other areas. In some states, a T was added for technology. That makes it the SBTDC with the same functions, but it has a group focusing on high-technology companies. The consultants in these organizations can assist and provide ideas to the business owner at no cost. This can be a great place to start the business planning process, and if there are areas these consultants cannot assist with, they can usually

recommend other professional resources to help the entrepreneur. One final resource is SCORE (www.score.org). This is an association of retired business owners and managers volunteering to assist businesses in their early stages of development.

Chapter 3 Review Questions

1. What policy friction do you have in your organization?

2. How does your continuous improvement planning include all employees?

3. Are your incentive programs aligned to maximize the benefit at your biggest constraint?

CHAPTER 4

Operating Expenses

Reduce Operating Expenses

Operating expenses are all the costs of running the business that do NOT vary directly with the products sold. These include all the Selling, General, and Administrative costs of the company not included in computing Value Added above, and may even include some manufacturing costs (rent, for example, is not usually dependent on the sales volume of the company). It also includes fixed cash obligations, such as the principal portion of debt payments. This gets away from Generally Accepted Accounting Principles, but we are gathering information to make internal decisions, not preparing a report for public viewing.

For those of you who are counting, you will see three sets of books for the company to maintain: one for the outside world (GAAP, soon to be the IFRS, International Financial Reporting Standards), one for the tax world, and one for internal use and decision- making. They reconcile to each other, and each has

CASH: MORE IS BETTER!

its own purpose and place. GAAP and tax policies do not always (that was polite for almost never) follow the "Five Laws of Cash" as explained in Chapter 1.

Reduce your costs!

1. Go to your current suppliers and firmly ask for a price reduction. You need to be willing to consider options your suppliers may give you, such as changing your schedules, or buying patterns (discussed above). You must be tough, but fair; they are likely to be in the same situation you are in.

2. Shop for new suppliers. Prepare a specification for suppliers to bid to. Keep the playing field level. Give your incumbent supplier every chance to keep your business – any new supplier needs to beat the champ! There is a cost to you every time you change a supplier, so there must be a cost or quality benefit to justify the change.

> Adding cost to inventory is not the same as adding value.

3. When you do add a new piece of equipment, negotiate hard with the vendor during the buying process. The vendor often has tools in their tool box to use to make the sale. These tools might include free training, spare parts, installation, reduced interest rate, free shipping, and other discounts. Some of these items have little or no additional costs to the vendor, but can save the buyer thousands of

dollars. Remember, the best time to negotiate is before you commit to buy.

4. Controlling Recurring Expenses

> **The best time to negotiate with a vendor is before you commit to buy.**

Every company that has been around for any length of time has them: contracts that automatically renew, unless you notify the supplier that you intend NOT to renew. These are common on copy machine maintenance, postage machine rental, factory linen supply, and a host of other items. Usually, buried on the fifth page of a seven- page contract will be a paragraph labeled "renewal notice" or some other innocent-sounding phrase. Upon reading the details, you will find that this three-year contract will automatically renew at the then current rates (disregard the deep discount you just negotiated)... unless you give them 60 days' written notice of your intent not to renew. Here is an example:

> Contract date: July 1, 2011
> Term: 36 months
> Automatic renewal date: June 30, 2014

They are required to tell you the above information. The missing critical two dates are:

- Notice date: April 30, 2014

- Start contract review process (Internal date): March 1, 2014

◄ CASH: MORE IS BETTER!

Armed with complete information, and being the well-organized person that you are, you have now given yourself 60 days to review the supplier's performance and get competitive bids if you choose to do so. Sixty days may not be the right number for every contract, so be sure to allocate enough calendar time to do a good job of vendor review and selection.

Every organization I have suggested this to has rebelled, saying they simply do not have enough time for this work. Every organization that has used this method has told me how much time it has actually saved them after the initial data is collected and organized. Most organizations end up organizing the vendor reviews into three-year cycles. This ensures that no vendor gets overlooked, but also does not require an annual review for the paper clip supplier.

Usually, the data is collected in a spreadsheet with columns like this:

- ➢ Vendor name – You may or may not organize the information alphabetically.

- ➢ Vendor number – This will help you get data from your system.

- ➢ Billing frequency – Annual, quarterly, or monthly are typical and will matter for your review cycles.

- ➢ Typical billing amount – this, along with the billing frequency, gives you a materiality range to help manage

OPERATING EXPENSES ➤

time. Smaller vendors doing a great job can get minimal reviews.

➢ General ledger number(s) – This not only helps find data, it helps organize amounts and work to not overload any area with work that is not material.

➢ Description – Briefly state what the contract is. Some vendors may have many contracts with your organization.

➢ Contract end date – Per the agreement.

➢ Contract notice date- Per the agreement.

➢ Review start date – A date you select as the minimum time needed to review the vendor's performance and do a competitive bidding process. Note: You may not do a serious competitive bidding process, but you <u>DO</u> want to communicate with the incumbent supplier in this time frame to negotiate a price better than the standard renewal rates.

➢ Department Responsibility – These decisions are best made by a team, including the main user of the service, the primary purchasing department, and the Controller. This team will weed out lazy reviews and keep the process honest.

➢ Responsible Person – The person primarily responsible for the success of the service under contract.

◄ CASH: MORE IS BETTER!

> ➤ Comments – relevant comments on the vendor, the review status, or other information to help from year to year.

After going through your expenditures for a period, you will find most of the vendor agreements to be put on the list. Don't be discouraged if a few stragglers show up later.

With this organized data in your pocket, and your team reviewing these agreements on a regular basis, you can feel confident that these potential cash leaks are being plugged.

5. Eliminate waste. Like recurring expenses, every company that has been around for a few years has something sloppy that they do, just because they always have done it that way. Get rid of it! No sacred cows allowed; they will poison the attitude of your staff in helping you save cash! There are companies that will review your purchases and recommend changes – and they get paid only by a percentage of the savings. No harm in talking to one of them. Consider these easy steps: turn machines off, water the lawn every other day, consolidate trips for supplies.

In the Lean World, a Kaizen event is held to eliminate waste. A Kaizen event is an intentional effort to understand the process, any process, at a very low level of detail. The process is defined and the operator is asked why each step is performed. Because the operator was told to perform it that way five years ago when he took that position is not a great reason to continue doing it that way. It is not uncommon for the operator to have ideas on how to make his

OPERATING EXPENSES

or her own job easier, but has not due to resistance from supervisors or other operators.

A kaizen event is a great time to review every step and to eliminate waste and processes. Do not make the mistake of doing a kaizen event only on the factory floor. Kaizen can be utilized in the office, sales, and marketing departments, and anywhere there are multiple steps and multiple people involved in completing a series of tasks. It is in everyone's interest to eliminate waste.

Care must be taken to assure people performing the tasks that if steps are eliminated, their jobs will not be in jeopardy. You cannot expect someone to make a suggestion that would eliminate their own job, or the job of the worker next to them, so you must convince them that not only will their job not be eliminated, but they will be rewarded for eliminating waste.

> **The Rate Is Too High!**
> Do not get caught in this trap!
> A $300 per hour attorney that takes an hour to do something costs less than a $200 per hour attorney that takes two hours for the same work. Likewise a $20 per hour welder that can really produce adds more value than a $15 per hour welder that causes a lot of rework.

Finally, you must actually cut the costs used to justify the project. Countless times I have heard complaints about cost savings promised by the "lean team" that did not seem to fall to the bottom line. After digging, what is usually found is that tough decisions promised are not completed. One example is the

◄ CASH: MORE IS BETTER!

justification that two operators will be eliminated when we buy this new machine – but they are merely transferred to other work stations, so the cost savings to the company is not realized. I always ask for names; if management will not put names on a sheet of paper while discussing the savings, they are not serious about cutting the cost. Another example is the assumption to sell an old machine after the new one is working. Time and again I find the old machine in the "bone yard" – just in case we need it! The cash assumed in the new machine justification does not materialize.

6. Check your utilities. Call your power company to be sure you are on the best tariff for the power load you are using now. Look for practices that may be wasting precious utilities, and see if there is a better way. If your operation has machines with large motors, it may be to your advantage to start those machines in sequence, thus drawing a small increase in power with each machine. Starting several machines at the same time will cause a large spike in power usage. Again, your electric company can assist you in understanding how your specific tariff affects your bill.

Reduce payroll costs.

7. Nobody likes to reduce staff, but occasionally it is required. Be sure you understand the tasks performed by everyone in the company. You do have up-to-date job descriptions, don't you? Take the work performed by the positions eliminated and move them to others who can absorb the work.

OPERATING EXPENSES

This is a tough job, but no one said running a company was easy.

Be sure to understand the work that each person had been doing that must be picked up by someone else. I use a tool I call a Staffing Matrix for this. It has all of the major tasks (such as Marketing planning, On time delivery, or New product development) in the left column and columns for each position on the team. Each item will have an R in it for the person responsible for that work. All the R tasks need to be assigned to someone who is capable and responsible and will carry them out. Sometimes I add a P for people who significantly participate in a task, and an S for people who will spend time supporting a task. There can be several P's and several S's on each line, but there can be only one R. This matrix can be used either to help develop job descriptions, or can be created from the existing job descriptions.

8. Reduce the rate of pay. This is another tough item to deal with. Hopefully this is an area where you have a history of leadership. In my opinion, ownership, followed by officers and other managers, should take the first and largest pay reductions. Leadership here will help the rest of the staff accept any reductions you are forced to make.

9. Reduce employee benefits. A benefit plan put together in the good times may not be appropriate in tough times. People have become accustomed to the benefits you have, so be careful and be fair. Take a survey of what is important to your employees to use as part of your decision-making

◄ CASH: MORE IS BETTER!

input. You might be surprised that a specific benefit is of little importance to many people but has a large cost associated with it. The survey is not the same as taking a vote, but it can help you to understand the needs of the people affected by your decisions and how to allocate cost to best meet those needs.

10. Have employees pay a larger share of the benefit package. Look at how you share costs now. Find out how other companies in your area, particularly competitors, handle benefits. Again, be fair. Consider the fairness of the cost of supplying family coverage to one person and the cost of supplying single coverage to the single person. Is there a better way?

Increasing the employee paid share of the benefit package has the same effect as a pay cut, so care must be taken to be fair. When a structural change to the benefit package takes place and affects current employees, it can create hard feelings, no matter how well-thought-out it is. However, two years from the decision, its sting will be a faded memory and new employees will think nothing of it. If it must be done, do it quickly, one time, and communicate all the reasons for making the changes.

At the time of this writing, all the changes required for small employers in the Affordable Care Act, also known as Obama Care, have not been fully defined. These will require fundamental changes to many companies' benefit plans and/or require companies with more than 50 employees to have some form of health insurance, or pay a penalty. Care must be taken to make good decisions relative to health care coverage and the overall benefit package for employees.

This is an evolving area with many core challenges to parts of the Affordable Care Act. Work with your insurance carrier and employees to understand all the impacts on your company and its employees. One last thing here-do not ignore the small business credit that is available to all employees beginning in 2011. Check with your tax advisor on maximizing this tax credit.

11. Shop for new benefit suppliers. This is a major factor affecting employee attitude, so do not do this often. Prepare a specification like what was discussed above and include your current provider. Consider self-insurance, if you are large enough, and have the financial discipline to manage the changes in cash flow.

12. Talk to your employees AND ALSO LISTEN TO YOUR EMPLOYEES. Let them know what is going on in the market, how it is affecting the company, and what you are looking at. Ask for their input. Show that you are sincerely listening and will give due consideration to any and all ideas. Give them feedback that you truly considered their comments even if they were not implemented.

Reduce interest expense by reducing debt.

13. Look at your cash management practices. Take any cash earning next to nothing in interest income, and pay down debt, especially credit cards or credit lines, that can be drawn on again if needed.

◄ CASH: MORE IS BETTER!

14. Convert debt to equity. This is a complicated issue, but eliminating the cash drain of principal and interest payments will free up precious cash to grow the company. Of course, the best value for the business needs to be documented in a thorough Business Plan to maximize the cash available for the shares sold.

15. Add equity. Selling a piece of the company is never easy, but if the plan shows that the pie will increase by more than the piece you are giving up, it may make sense.

Chapter 4 Review Questions

1. Have you done your kaizen events at the biggest constraint?

2. Have you reviewed your supply chain for cost and time savings opportunities?

3. Have you reviewed your maintenance and support contracts to avoid automatic renewals (at outrageous pricing!)?

CHAPTER 5

Investment

Reduce Investment in Working Capital and Fixed Assets

If Cash is King, then Working Capital is the rest of the royal court. Working Capital is simply Current Assets minus Current Liabilities. More is better. An Asset or Liability is Current if it can be turned to cash or will require cash in the next twelve months. Fixed Assets are those expected to last more than a year and get depreciated over their useful life. Investments in Fixed Assets require cash or debt to purchase.

Reduce your demands on Cash

1. Reduce your Days Sales Outstanding. This is computed as Accounts Receivable divided by Sales per day (or the last month) on an annualized basis. Smaller is better.

    Do NOT congratulate yourself if you discover that you are better than an industry average. Work to be the best in class! Call slow-pay customers, because it is the squeaky wheel

CASH: MORE IS BETTER!

that gets paid. On big invoices, call before they are due to be sure they are approved and scheduled for payment.

2. Consider factoring your Accounts Receivable. This is where someone buys your Accounts Receivable at a discount. You make slightly less money, but you get paid now and sometimes remove the risk of eventual nonpayment by your customer. This does not work for everyone, but it is certainly worth looking into. Usually, you will need to change the "Pay To" instructions with your customer to have their check sent directly to the Factor. This is difficult for many companies to deal with, but can relieve the cash strain for a time. Also, note that this is a one-time improvement in cash that will reverse itself if you go back to traditional collection procedures.

3. Do you have some lazy cash? Lazy Cash includes old Accounts Receivable, obsolete Inventory, small remaining balances on cash accounts that are not used anymore, and underutilized equipment, just to name a few items. Clean these items up. It will simplify your Balance Sheet and create space in your plant.

4. Do not buy raw materials until you need them. Work with your vendors. See if they will make your parts and deliver them as needed. Paying slightly more may be better than holding inventory.

5. Don't perform operations on parts until you need to. Be practical here; starting and stopping may be counterproductive. Inventory has little real value until someone wants

INVESTMENT

to buy it from you. Smaller lot sizes increases set-ups, but often have very small costs compared to the benefit of having parts when you need them.

6. As a last resort, extend payments to your suppliers. The consequences of this are lost trust, being placed on COD, losing a priority position with that supplier, and possibly having the supplier choose to stop doing business with you. Be sure you can keep any promises for payment you make to a supplier.

7. Postpone asset additions. This seems obvious, but takes a disciplined approach to accomplish in some organizations. You may have a long- standing policy of replacing PCs every three years. Someone needs to decide to extend that to save the cash – of course, that is assuming the repair costs and potential productivity issues will be less than the prorated asset costs. Get out your pencils and keep them sharp!

8. If you must add an asset, consider leasing instead of buying. Certain high- technology assets are often better to lease than to buy, but other assets may not be. In tight cash circumstances, however, the smaller down payment and other leasing advantages often tip the scales toward leasing. Leasing is generally more expensive over the life of the lease, but if credit is tight, keeping the obligation off the Balance Sheet with a lease may be a great option.

9. Contact your debt holders and arrange to pay interest only for a period of time. This may take some tough negotiations,

◄ CASH: MORE IS BETTER!

but the cash freed up may be critical to the survival of the operation.

Chapter 5 Review Questions

1. Where do you have lazy cash lying around that could be put to better use?

2. Is your fixed asset addition plan reasonable for the current times?

3. Is your Days Sales Outstanding where you need it to be?

CHAPTER 6

Manage Better

Some items fit into one or more categories, or need to be looked at when you are completely out of your comfort zone.

Some such things to look at include:

1. <u>Advisory Boards.</u> Everybody needs a friend to talk to from time to time. If you don't have one, find one. Start an Advisory Board or join a peer group to share your issues with other business people who can help you think through tough issues. Not only do entrepreneurs often not have a trusted advisor, they may have no accountability to meeting goals or staying the course. This is where an Advisory Board, or at least a trusted advisor, will help the entrepreneur set goals - and keep them. I am a big fan of Advisory Boards. When done well, they help management develop their thoughts and become better managers and planners. They do take time to prepare, and that preparation is what makes them so valuable.

2. <u>Barter.</u> Have you considered bartering for certain items? There are organizations that set up trades between two or more parties. This can be a great way to move unwanted inventory or other assets to markets that will not upset your pricing strategy in existing markets.

3. <u>Maintenance Agreements.</u> Watch your maintenance agreements and routine overhead contracts. As discussed in Chapter 4, these include items like copy machines, trash collection, uniform laundering, and so on. List specific dates for renewal and for notice on all contracts, like waste disposal, copier maintenance, and my favorite: the postage machine. Many times these contracts will state that you must notify the supplier 60 or 90 days before the renewal date or the contract automatically renews at whatever the new rates are! Sort by notice date and make sure you send a letter to the supplier stating that you intend to shop for options.

    It probably does not make sense to review every one of these every year. Organizing these into efforts that can be completed once every three years may make some sense for your organization. So unless the vendor has a noticeable change in cost or performance, you may not review that contract for three years. Most of these contracts are not large enough to justify the annual review time, but even the smallest one is too large to ignore.

4. <u>Budgets.</u> Revise your business plan and budgets. If you are way off, don't beat yourself up for the next six months! Set a new target based on the new circumstances, and go beat that target!

MANAGE BETTER ▶

This is a hard one for some managers to deal with. If your goal at the beginning of the year was $1 million a month, and for some reason the next six months looks like half of that is a best-case scenario, change the plan. Organize around something that's achievable, and celebrate when you do better rather than beat yourself up every month for being so far off target. This will make your plans believable, and the cash flow projections-both incoming and outgoing-will match reality.

Likewise, if the next six months look like $2 million a month is possible, change the plan. Celebrate the increase, and create a plan based on the new reality. Then get to work and do even better than that.

5. Smile! Don't get into the "woe is me" funk when times seem tough. Put a smile on your face. Accept the challenge. You have an amazing amount of power. The act of doing one little thing can start a momentum shift-in attitude if not in fact. Attitude goes a long way to getting the real momentum on your side, too.

It is easy to say "The market stinks; what can I do?" Well, you can adjust. Sell service instead of hardware. Sell in units of one instead of 10. Do something positive. Momentum is a great thing – get it moving in your direction.

6. Credit Card Purchases. Use credit cards to buy things. I cannot believe I said that. Avoid this as long as you can. This sometimes adds 30 days to the cash float without

adding interest. This works only if you pay them off every month! Otherwise, this will get <u>very</u> expensive.

7. <u>Credit Card Sales.</u> Use credit cards to receive payments from customers. There is a small fee for this, but many businesses find this easier than writing a check. Another advantage is that the customer can act immediately by making a payment while on the phone instead of relying on them to actually prepare and mail the check as they promised to do.

8. <u>Estimated Tax Payments.</u> Check your state and federal tax estimated payments. If your current reality is different than the projection used to make the estimates, you certainly should consider lowering the rest of your payments. You may even look into getting a refund of the estimates already paid for the current year. Make a regular meeting time with your tax advisor at least three months prior to year end to be sure to take advantage of any special tax situations available to the company.

9. <u>Insurance Based on Sales or Payroll.</u> Look at your payments for liability, workers' compensation, and any other insurance based on payroll or sales. It is usually easy to adjust these estimated premiums and reduce your future payments and/or get some money back from earlier payments.

10. <u>Surcharges for Freight.</u> Look hard at freight surcharges. Everybody is doing this lately, and if you pay the freight, you need to pay for the increased fuel costs. You do have the right to understand how the surcharge is calculated, to

see how it moves up and down, and to review these occasionally. Also, if your purchase agreement is a price that includes freight, and the vendor adds a surcharge, which is a price increase, you have the right to reject and renegotiate. Again, don't be pigheaded about it; you need to be fair with the supplier. Get them to explain how the surcharge works, and negotiate the fee with them like any other price increase.

11. <u>Partner.</u> Look for ways to partner or joint venture with another business. This can reduce your costs and risks, while maintaining your upside potential in many cases. Get creative. Look for someone buying similar raw materials but selling a different product or to a different market.

> **Go improve something!**

As you can see, there are many ways to change things in your business. Some will be improvements. Some will have negative consequences. Some will do little or nothing. Choosing what to do and when is key and understanding how decisions made in accounting, or in operations, affect cash flow is a good perspective to have.

Another observation is that business decisions, like life decisions, are not made in isolation. When you make one decision, say to bundle two items at a discounted price, it is part of all the decisions you have made to that point. Your competition is making decisions at the same time; they might outflank you for a moment and win a battle. You then need to erase the white

CASH: MORE IS BETTER!

board and create another opportunity for your customer that the competition will find hard to match.

What is the biggest mistake entrepreneurs make regarding cash management?

This is the last of the five Frequently Asked Questions about Cash I listed in the Introduction. As you can imagine, there is a long list of questions and determining the "biggest" is hard because the circumstances vary so much. So here is a short list of errors that are seen over and over again.

- Spending money on nice to have, but not necessary things. I once witnessed the owners, who had worked for a company for about ten years and then purchased it, upgrade their cars, computers, phones, desks, and so on. They wanted to show the world that they had arrived. Those costs, plus the debt service from the acquisition, crippled the cash flow of the company for over two years.

- Trusting employees too much. When the business starts to grow and the layers start to form, it is hard to keep your fingers in every pie without being accused of micromanaging. When it comes to managing cash, you must. Too many headlines tell stories of trusted employees who has been stealing from their companies-sometimes for years. Employees also buy personal items on company credit cards; when caught, they always say they meant to pay it back. Part of your responsibility is to protect company assets. You need to review monthly bank statements, ask questions when things don't look right, maybe even have the bank statements sent to your personal attention and review them from time to time. You need to set the standard for integrity if you expect your employees to respect the assets of the company.

- Treating the business as their personal toy. Even if yours is a "lifestyle" business, the people who work there see it as their source of income and should take pride in doing a great job. If you divert company energies to your personal projects and then wonder why a shipment is late, or then say you cannot afford to give raises, expect there to be some disgruntled employees. Shop employees sometimes take tools and sell scrap – often because they have seen the owner do it! If you as the owner do not respect the business, as a business, it will be difficult for employees to respect the business and be diligent about making it a success.

Oh, I am sure there are more, but you get the idea. A business is a beautiful thing. Treat it with respect and dignity, and it can provide you with all the benefits you desire. Treat it as a means to an end, and it just might disappear – remember the goose and the golden egg story? It is about business – your business.

Give your business the love and attention it deserves, and it can help you attain your professional and personal goals and have a great time doing it. Treat your customers, employees, and suppliers well and they will work hard to deliver their

CASH: MORE IS BETTER!

piece of your success. We are all in this together, and together we can achieve great things.

For cash, that great thing is very simple –

Cash: More Is Better!

It is my sincere hope that this list of ideas is relevant to your organization and will be referred to often as your real-world situation changes.

Chapter 6 Action Items:
1. Do you have a friend or advisor(s) to talk to?

2. Do you use your budgets and projections to communicate and motivate?

3. Do you show your optimism for the future by wearing a smile?

CHAPTER 7

Personal Reflections on Decisions

Well, there you have it-more than 50 ways to conserve cash or improve your business situation. I am sure there are other great suggestions, too. Please send me your thoughts to add to this list. Send your comments to Fred@CashMIB.com or comment on the website: CashMIB.com.

As a planner by nature, I am always making lists, comparing the pros and cons of a situation, and applying logic to the decision at hand. There are certainly decisions to be made where that works well.

When it comes to *Cash: More Is Better* – that goes without saying. The make or buy decision is one that can be calculated with the right data. To expand into city A vs city B is more complex, but can still be looked at with rows and columns of data and combination of facts and assumptions. Decisions of principle are often not so easy.

Within the business, decisions that do not lend themselves to spreadsheet analysis include things like:

CASH: MORE IS BETTER!

- Which person to hire?
- How many times do you overlook mistakes during a training period for a new employee?
- How much credit do you give a new customer?
- How much credit do you give a good, long-term customer who has become a slow-pay account?

For those questions, and a zillion more like them, having a clear understanding of the vision, mission, and objectives of the company is required to make decisions that are consistent and will move the company in the right direction.

On the personal side, in my career I have found that weighing the priorities of business and life to be a constant challenge. The standard response is God first, family second, and job third. That is easy to say and extremely hard to do and the response varies depending on the circumstances. The decision that was made when the children were preschool age may not be right when they are in middle school or high school. Some personal decisions can be very complex and reveal conflicts between career objectives and family objectives, such as:

- Should I accept a great job opportunity requiring a move?
- Should I "cook the books just a little" to make my boss look good?
- Should I start a new business?

PERSONAL REFLECTIONS ON DECISIONS

- Should I become an Elder at church or coach my son's soccer team, or do both?

Providing for the family will always be a high priority. Having a great job (or a great company) might be the means to provide for the family. That job, however, sometimes requires excessive hours or travel that reduces the time available to be with the family. Yet spending quality time with the family pays more long-term dividends than a comfortable bank balance. So there is the classic dilemma: Working hard to provide for the family causes tension because you cannot spend enough quality time with the family.

Scheduling family time is important. Yet you cannot schedule an hour of 'quality time' from 6 to 7 p.m. on Wednesday night. Quality time just does not work that way. Spending time with the family on things important to THEM is one key to quality time. Another key is quantity of time. When your family knows that what is important to them is important to you, those quality moments happen. So put time with the family on your calendar and treat it with the same respect you do your business meetings.

Again, having a clear understanding of your family vision, mission, and objectives will determine how you decide these complex issues. The answer to that dilemma for me has always come after much soul-searching and prayer. If you really believe that God is the provider of your daily bread, then put your faith to work and spend time in His Word listening to His voice of wisdom and comfort. Work hard, "as for the Lord." As it says in Colossians 3:17 "And whatever you do, whether in word or

◄ CASH: MORE IS BETTER!

deed, do it all in the name of the Lord Jesus, giving thanks to God the Father through him"-and all the other parts of life will take care of themselves.

Now go save come cash - because when it comes to

Cash: More Is Better!

www.ingramcontent.com/pod-product-compliance
Lightning Source LLC
Chambersburg PA
CBHW030910180526
45163CB00004B/1777